Not by Bread Alone

Daily Reflections for Lent 2007

Sherri L. Vallee

LITURGICAL PRESS
Collegeville, Minnesota

www.litpress.org

Nihil Obstat: Rev. Robert C. Harren, J.C.L. *Censor deputatus*
Imprimatur: ✠ Most Rev. John F. Kinney, J.C.D., D.D., Bishop of St. Cloud, Minnesota, May 17, 2006

Cover design by Ann Blattner

1	2	3	4	5	6	7	8

ISSN: 1550-803X

ISBN-13: 978-0-8146-2991-8
ISBN-10: 0-8146-2991-1

Introduction

As we begin our Lenten journey, let us take a few moments to gaze at the scene depicted on the cover of this book. The photo captures desert sands blown by the wind. In the distance, we see a mountain against the horizon. Our Lenten experience is shaped by time spent in the desert, without ever losing sight of the mountain.

Those who climb mountains must have self-discipline and steadfast determination. They push themselves throughout their journey, sacrificing personal comfort in their efforts to reach their goal. They yearn to experience the exhilarating feeling that will come with the view from the mountaintop. Throughout our Lenten journey, we too climb the mountain. Like mountain-climbers, we might sacrifice some personal comfort, perhaps giving up leisure time in order to help others. God shows us the path and guides our footsteps. We yearn for the goal: we long to celebrate the joy of Easter, to relish in the glory of the resurrection on the mountaintop. It is this vision that propels us forward as we devote ourselves to prayer, to works of charity, and to listening more intently to the word of God.

Desert experiences have set the stage for critical moments of growth throughout our salvation history. The Israelites spent forty years in the desert after God freed them from Egypt. Forty years passed before they were able to enter the land of milk and honey. It was a time of development, a time for them to be formed into a people, into God's people.

Desert experiences take us away from our everyday routine, remove us from distractions, and foster a deeper awareness of God. The psalmist cries out to God: "O God, you are my God— / for you I long! / For you my body yearns; / for you my soul thirsts / Like a land parched, lifeless, / and without water" (Ps 63:1). In the dry and weary land of the Lenten experience, we deepen our awareness of how much our souls truly crave oneness with God. It is an act of love for God to take us into the desert, to give us this opportunity to grow and become the people that we are meant to be. May we embrace this privileged time wholeheartedly.

As we set out on this desert journey, we remind ourselves of the Easter joy that awaits us. But there will also be joy in the desert, throughout this Lenten journey, for God is with us. This time of reflection may lead us to new insights. We may become more aware of God's plan for our lives. As God nudges us to greater self-awareness, we will recognize areas where we have failed as individuals or as a community. Recognizing one's failures is not pleasant, but when we seek reconciliation we will be amazed by the depth of God's compassion and love. Reconciliation is truly something to celebrate.

After his baptism, before beginning his public ministry, Jesus spent forty days in the desert and practiced self-denial. Hungry and weak, when the tempter urged him to change stones into bread, Jesus responded, "One does not live by bread alone, / but by every word that comes from the mouth of God" (Matt 4:4).

During this Lent, may we also turn our wholehearted attention to every word that comes from the mouth of God and allow it to speak to our hearts. This book is structured around the daily readings for Eucharist and may be used either individually or for group reflection. Readers are encouraged to read the Scripture passages in their entirety. Some may find this to be a useful way of preparing for daily Eucharist or for further reflection following the celebration of the Eucharist.

I dedicate this book to my loving parents, Vern and Betty Vallee.

Writing this book has been a great privilege, and I cherish the opportunity it has afforded me to reflect more deeply on the word of God. My sincere thanks go out to friends, family, students, and professors who prayed for me and cheered me on as this deadline approached.

I offer a heartfelt prayer for all who will use this book. Let us pray for each other. May we all set out on this journey with open hearts and eager anticipation of the growth and transformation that God will effect in each and every one of us this Lent.

On a Journey

Readings: Joel 2:12-18; 2 Cor 5:20–6:2; Matt 6:1-6, 16-18

Scripture:
Even now, says the LORD,
   return to me with your whole heart,
   with fasting, and weeping, and mourning;
Rend your hearts, not your garments,
   and return to the LORD, your God. (Joel 2:12-13)

Reflection: Every autumn, millions of salmon battle their way back to the stream where their lives began—leaping waterfalls and overcoming rapids, drawn by a force far greater than themselves—to lay their eggs for the next generation. We too are drawn by a force far greater than ourselves toward the source of all creation. We are drawn toward God. God is yearning for our return. Unlike the salmon, though, we may choose whether or not to pursue the journey, whether or not to respond to God's call.

Joel's plea is for an earnest yes in response to that call. He calls on us to rend our hearts. The heart in Hebrew thought was not only the seat of emotion but also the seat of the will. We must make a heartfelt decision to return to God.

Our journey is not solitary. We look around the church on Ash Wednesday and see that we are not alone. Ash Wednesday is one of the most well-attended weekday liturgies, responding to a deep need to begin Lent well. The whole church is going on retreat for the next forty days, a journey of prayer, almsgiving, fasting, examination of conscience, and reconciliation. We are journeying as a community of believers. Like the salmon's journey, ours is one of homecoming, a journey that may cause us to confront some obstacles, but a journey that will bring us to great joy. We are coming home, where we belong. We are preparing for Easter glory.

Meditation: What aspect of my interpersonal relationships, prayer life, attitudes, or behavior needs my greatest attention this Lent? I turn that over to God and pray for the grace to journey forward during these forty days.

Prayer: Earnest and loving God, you call all people to yourself. You call us to authenticity and honesty. Draw us closer to yourself. Allow us to deepen our faith this Lent, to grow more intimately in relationship with you, and to live as you desire. For this we pray, in the name of Jesus, who calls us to new life. Amen.

A Model Answer

Readings: 1 Pet 5:1-4; Matt 16:13-19

Scripture:
He said to them, "But who do you say that I am?"
Simon Peter said in reply,
  "You are the Christ, the Son of the living God."
    (Matt 16:15-16)

Reflection: "Who do you say that I am?" Matthew, Mark, and Luke all describe Jesus asking his disciples this very question. How would we respond? How do we understand Jesus?

Perhaps the answer varies at different points in our faith journey. Some no doubt have turned to Christianity out of respect for Jesus as a great teacher. Some have accepted him as a prophet. But to really follow Jesus, we ultimately need to give the same answer as Simon Peter. We need to recognize Jesus as the Christ, the Messiah, and the Son of God.

Simon Peter's answer expresses two profound truths. The word "Christ" literally means "anointed." The corresponding word of Hebrew origin is "messiah." A messiah was a human being, uniquely chosen and anointed by God to fulfill a royal or priestly ministry. The people of Israel were awaiting the promised Messiah, the Christ, the long-expected king of the House of David. In declaring that Jesus was Son of the living God, Simon Peter was affirming Jesus' divinity.

Both human and divine dimensions are key to understanding who Jesus is.

If both dimensions are not seen in balance, our prayer and our attitudes can become skewed. For example, we might place so much emphasis on Jesus' humanity that we fail to recognize his power to change our lives. Or, we might forget that Jesus came to earth as a human being born of Mary and think of him as only divine. This might lead us to be hesitant to come to him in prayer, forgetting that he has shared our human experience, that he understands our struggles and welcomes us with open arms. We must never lose sight of both aspects of Christ's identity.

Today's gospel challenges us to be more like Simon Peter—and more like Christ himself. Simon Peter's answer, cultivated through a loving relationship, is indeed worthy of praise. May our relationship with Christ enable us to deepen and clarify our perception of Christ's identity. We were anointed at our baptism and confirmation and are privileged to be sons and daughters of God. May our lives conform ever more closely to that of Jesus, the Son of the living God.

Meditation: How do I answer when Jesus asks me, "Who do you say that I am?" How do I perceive Jesus? What is Christ's role in my life today?

Prayer: Come Holy Spirit, enkindle in me a burning desire to grow in my love and knowledge of Jesus as Christ and Son of God. Guide my prayer. Lead me to respond to Jesus with the same recognition and confidence as Simon Peter did. Amen.

A Worthy Fast

Readings: Isa 58:1-9a; Matt 9:14-15

Scripture:
This, rather, is the fasting that I wish:
   releasing those bound unjustly,
   untying the thongs of the yoke;
Setting free the oppressed,
   breaking every yoke;
Sharing your bread with the hungry,
   sheltering the oppressed and the homeless;
Clothing the naked when you see them,
   and not turning your back on your own.
Then light shall break forth like the dawn,
   and your wound shall quickly be healed. (Isa 58:6-8)

Reflection: The French explorer, Jacques Cartier (1491–1557), made three voyages to North America between 1534 and 1547, trying to discover a Northwest Passage to the Orient. While he is credited as a great explorer, he never found the Northwest Passage. Along the way he was overjoyed to discover diamonds and gold, which later turned out to be quartz and fool's gold, a second source of disappointment.

   At times, we may think that we are going in the right direction and doing the right thing; but, like the early explorers, we may be operating with limited vision. Maybe we are pleased with fool's gold rather than continuing our quest for something more authentic.

Today's reading from Isaiah draws our attention to such misguided efforts. The people were fasting and praying, and they expected God to shower them with blessings in return. But they were quarrelling, fighting, and paying no attention whatsoever to those in need. God sent Isaiah to draw their attention to the injustices all around them.

Unlike Cartier and other early explorers, we have a map to guide us. We have the gospel to teach us, and we have the Holy Spirit dwelling in our hearts. We also have the church community to discern with us the needs of the world. If we are attentive, we will be led to notice those around us who are in need, and we will be moved to take action. This, indeed, will be pleasing to God.

Meditation: How is the Holy Spirit prompting me to address the needs of those around me? How is my fasting affecting my awareness of the needs of others? Am I satisfied with false idols like fool's gold rather than seeking God's will for my life?

Prayer: God of justice, I praise and thank you for moments of insight when you open my eyes and push me forward to care for others. Thank you for sending the Holy Spirit to guide me. Bless all those in need. Amen.

February 24: Saturday after Ash Wednesday

Like a Physician

Readings: Isa 58:9b-14; Luke 5:27-32

Scripture:
Jesus said to them in reply,
  "Those who are healthy do not need a physician, but the
    sick do.
I have not come to call the righteous to repentance but
    sinners." (Luke 5:31-32)

Reflection: Posters for the 1970 movie, *Love Story,* coined the expression, "Love means never having to say you're sorry." What a false notion! In all but the most superficial of human relationships, we need to say "I'm sorry" on a fairly regular basis. We all have human weaknesses, and we know that it is impossible to spend time with others without occasionally doing or saying something that we later regret.

Parents usually teach children from a very young age to say "I'm sorry." Even before they can tell the difference between an accident and a deliberate act, children know that it is appropriate to say "I'm sorry" when they break somebody's toy or disobey a request. The good habit of being honest enough to admit fault begins early.

Wise parents also model another very good habit. When somebody hurts them and apologizes, they respond, "I forgive you." Or maybe they indicate their openness to reconciliation by saying, "That's okay—don't worry about it."

Those simple words are a sign of grace, healing the wounds caused by sin and restoring relationships. When we forgive one another, we are following Jesus' model of forgiving sinners. We do not act as judge before our friends and loved ones, but as healer. We experience healing when we free ourselves of guilt by acknowledging our failings, and we experience and convey healing when we have the strength to say, "I forgive you." It is a sign of grace when we can honestly forgive and let go of past hurts.

Jesus, as a physician who heals the sick, recognizes that sin exists in our world and in our relationships, and he calls us all to repentance. We are comforted when we think of Jesus as healer. Some of us hesitate before calling our physician, perhaps because we do not want to be seen as a hypochondriac, bothering the doctor for something insignificant. But we know that the physician often can diagnose our ailment and prescribe a remedy. When our hearts are moved to repentance, we need not hesitate before turning to Jesus, our healer. The remedy, the grace of forgiveness and the comforting embrace of reconciliation, is freely given and will make us well.

Meditation: In what ways am I called to be a light to others, offering or facilitating the healing that forgiveness brings? In what ways am I in need of the healing grace of forgiveness?

Prayer: God of light and healing, grant me the honesty to be able to admit my own failings. Allow your light to shine in the dark moments of my life and bring healing. Amen.

Milk and Honey

Readings: Deut 26:4-10; Rom 10:8-13; Luke 4:1-13

Scripture:
He brought us out of Egypt
　with his strong hand and outstretched arm,
　with terrifying power, with signs and wonders;
　and bringing us into this country,
　he gave us this land flowing with milk and honey.
　　(Deut 26:8-9)

Reflection: Our lives have ups and downs. Sometimes we get into a rut or we feel dejected, and everything seems to be going wrong. The struggles can seem never ending. Then something strikes us—a kind word, a favorite hymn, a sunny day, or an unexpected event touches our heart and offers us a new perspective. At times, things simply improve and we cannot put our finger on the reason. Such life experiences give us reason to have hope whenever things are not going well. Things have improved before and things will improve again. God is good.

For the people of Israel, the desert journey lasted a lifetime, a time full of struggles and dangers. But God sustained them on this journey and ultimately lavished generosity on them. They arrived in a land of milk and honey, receiving more than they had ever dreamed possible.

In third-century North Africa, and a bit later in Rome, we know that when adults were baptized, anointed, and welcomed to the eucharistic table for the first time, they were given a drink of milk and honey before they received the Eucharist itself. While this drink might be symbolic of baby food, recognizing the baby steps that the newly baptized were taking on their faith journey, it is also related to today's Scripture and the land of milk and honey. After a period of intense preparation for baptism, much like our Lent today, the newly baptized in the early church had arrived at the Promised Land, and were able to literally experience a taste of what God had in store for them in the Eucharist.

At our baptism, and each time that we come to the eucharistic banquet, we also gain a taste of the bounty that God has in store for us.

Meditation: When I am feeling down, how does God lift my spirits? What gives me hope and strength during the desert periods of my life? When my life begins to improve, and I find myself showered with many blessings, do I recognize and give thanks for God's "strong hand and outstretched arm" in my life?

Prayer: Lord, God of transformation, through your death and resurrection you have transformed the world. Transform my heart this day. Lift me up and enable me to see how you are at work in my life. Amen.

Relationships

Readings: Lev 19:1-2, 11-18; Matt 25:31-46

Scripture:
You shall not bear hatred for your brother in your heart.
Though you may have to reprove him,
   do not incur sin because of him.
Take no revenge and cherish no grudge
   against your fellow countrymen.
You shall love your neighbor as yourself.
   I am the LORD. (Lev 19:17-18)

Reflection: Interpersonal issues are likely the most common sin with which most of us grapple. From the time we are young children and confess, "I hit my brother when he broke my toy," our sinful actions are often related to the ways that we react to the actions of others.

At an assertive training workshop several years ago, I learned that there are three classic ways of responding when others hurt us. One extreme is to be aggressive, responding angrily and forcefully to every minor discretion. Not good. Another extreme is to be passive, to not acknowledge that the other person's words or actions have bothered us, to try to ignore or forget what has happened. Over time, there is a danger that resentment can build inside us because the issue has not been addressed. The in-between response, the one that psychologists tell us is generally the most healthy, is to be honest and assertive, letting the other person know that we feel hurt—and then gently, politely requesting a change in behavior. This kind of openness is difficult and may leave us vulnerable, but it can also be a liberating step toward a better relationship.

Relationships with certain people can challenge us, but they help hone our ability to interact and to cope. When we try to see Christ in one another, when we pray for one another, dialogue flows more easily.

Meditation: Is there somebody in my life toward whom I bear a grudge? Do I wish for vengeance against any person or organization? If so, what is the root cause? Have I prayed about it? Have I prayed for the person who has hurt me? What can I do to free myself from this burden? How can I truly love my neighbor?

Prayer: God of relationships, you sent your only Son to become truly human, to experience human emotions and interactions. Allow us to follow his example of love. Give us wisdom and generosity of heart so that we may truly love one another as you commanded. We ask this through your Son, our Lord. Amen.

The Lord's Prayer

Readings: Isa 55:10-11; Matt 6:7-15

Scripture:
Our Father who art in heaven,
   hallowed be thy name. (Matt 6:10a)

Reflection: The Lord's Prayer contains such familiar words. But do we stop to really pay attention to the words we pray? Do we allow their significance to penetrate our heart?

When we pray "Our Father," we are exercising a privilege. Through our baptism, we have become adopted daughters and sons of God, and so Jesus teaches us that we have the privilege to address God in a most intimate way. We are free to address God tenderly and confidently, as a child would approach a parent. We share this privilege with all Christians, and so we pause to pray for Christians of all denominations throughout the world who might be praying together with us. United by God, we form a single family of believers.

Indeed, we have the privilege to call God "Father," and with privilege comes responsibility. When we pray the Lord's Prayer, we are reminded of our duty to live as sons and daughters of God. As members of the church, we are called to be God's presence for others; so whenever we pray this prayer, we ask for guidance to do so.

In John's Gospel, when Jesus is preparing to die, he cries out, "Father, glorify your name." The response from God is: "I have glorified it and will glorify it again" (John 12:28). Christ's life, death, and resurrection is a glorification of God's name. Through our baptism and our participation in the Eucharist we enter into the dying and rising of Christ—and we too glorify God's name. Our ongoing growth in faith is, in itself, a hallowing and praising of God's name.

Meditation: Let us pause for a moment simply to praise God's holy name.

Prayer: Our Father, thank you for choosing us as your children. Thank you for sending your Son to reveal yourself to us and your Spirit to make us aware of your presence and action in our lives. Bless all people throughout the world, that we may be united in working for the coming of your kingdom. We ask this through your Son and our Lord, Jesus Christ. Amen.

Repent

Readings: Jonah 3:1-10; Luke 11:29-32

Scripture:
When the news reached the king of Nineveh,
　he rose from his throne, laid aside his robe,
　covered himself with sackcloth, and sat in the ashes.
　　(Jonah 3:6)

Reflection: The reaction of the king of Nineveh is remarkable. How many of us would immediately repent when someone points out our wrongdoing? How many of us would even acknowledge our wrongdoing? Would we not argue or become defensive or try to blame someone else? Would we not be tempted to deny any involvement or responsibility?

The king's reaction is all the more remarkable given that he was not part of the people of Israel. On the contrary, Nineveh was the capital of Assyria, the enemy who had conquered the northern kingdom of Israel two centuries earlier. Jonah was proclaiming repentance in this community very reluctantly, not really wanting God's love to extend to those who had caused so much pain in the past. If the king of Nineveh, who was not part of God's chosen people, can repent so readily, what prevents us from finding the humility to do the same?

Every day, we hear about the damage being done to the environment by our use of fossil fuels, our farming processes, our volume of garbage, and our destruction of forests. We see vivid images of violence and suffering in other parts of the world. What is our response to this news?

When we meditate prayerfully on Scripture, or when we listen attentively to the word of God proclaimed in the midst of the worshiping assembly, something touches our hearts. The word of God impinges on our lives, making us more aware of the effects of our action or our inaction on the lives of others. How ready are we to open our minds, our hearts, and our ears to truly listen? How willing are we to repent and amend our lifestyles?

Meditation: God's loving kindness extends to all. Mindful of the immensity of God's mercy, let us examine our hearts. To what personal or communal sin is God drawing my attention this day? What aspect of my life, or of the life of my society, demands repentance and change?

Prayer: God of mercy, open my eyes and my ears to truly see and hear your message in my life this day. Show me where I need to repent. Show me how you are calling me to change and to grow. Grant me the humility to acknowledge sin and the willingness to take the first steps toward change. Guide my thoughts and actions this day. This is my heartfelt prayer. Amen.

March 1: Thursday of the First Week of Lent

God's Generosity

Readings: Esth C:12, 14-16, 23-25; Matt 7:7-12

Scripture:
Ask and it will be given to you;
   seek and you will find;
   knock and the door will be opened to you.
For everyone who asks, receives; and the one who seeks,
    finds;
   and to the one who knocks, the door will be opened.
   (Matt 7:7-8)

Reflection: While on a bus tour of Ireland and Northern Ireland a few years ago, I became fascinated by the sheep. Lambs and sheep were everywhere: crossing the roads, climbing rocky cliffs overlooking the North Sea, wandering in search of grass, and sometimes getting caught in brambles or fences. They enjoyed tremendous freedom but were also in need of their shepherd's guiding hand.

We too are in need of our Shepherd's assistance and guidance. We sometimes find our lives to be a source of chaos, with many conflicting responsibilities and difficult decisions. We yearn for a guiding hand, someone to show us the way, to bring order out of the chaos of our lives.

Sometimes, when I feel particularly overloaded, when I have so much on my plate that I cannot figure out where to start, I waste time fretting over the workload rather than getting at it and starting somewhere. This feeling of being in disarray is particularly evident when I have not paused to pray for guidance. When I pause to pray, I feel centered and reassured and can get started on whatever needs my attention.

Meditation: What are the needs in my life? In what areas of my life should I turn to God for guidance?

Prayer: Generous and loving God, you know our innermost thoughts and needs. Direct our minds and hearts. Continue to invite us to respond to your love. We praise you for your unfathomable generosity and attentiveness to our every need. We pray this through Jesus Christ our Lord, in the unity of the Holy Spirit. Amen.

Anger and Forgiveness

Readings: Ezek 18:21-28; Matt 5:20-26

Scripture:
But I say to you, whoever is angry with his brother
  will be liable to judgment,
  and whoever says to his brother, *Raqa,*
  will be answerable to the Sanhedrin,
  and whoever says, "You fool," will be liable to fiery
    Gehenna. (Matt 5:22)

Reflection: In this passage Jesus is extending the traditional Law. Following Jesus involves something deeper than obeying the commandments. In this case he is elaborating on the commandment, "You shall not kill." Anger, if not curbed, can be just as significant as murder. What a scary thought! Judgment (or the local court), the Sanhedrin, and Gehenna would all be connected with trying a case of murder. Can anger really be just as severe in its consequences?

Anger can certainly cause us to say or do things that we later regret. It can lead to harsh words, hard feelings, desires for revenge—and can ultimately lead to hostility and warfare. We can become obsessed in reflecting on the way that another person has treated us. Anger can consume us and harm our relationships with others.

At times, of course, anger is very understandable. When we discover that someone has been abandoned or injured by another, we feel outrage. When we become aware of injustice in our communities, we feel moved to speak out. The key is to channel that emotion and to seek both justice and reconciliation.

We are called to be one. Jesus tells us that we must be reconciled with one another before bringing our gifts to the altar. This is one reason that historically in some places the sign of peace occurred before the gifts were brought to the altar (rather than at its current place in the Eucharist). We cannot be a truly eucharistic people if we are divided and angry. We are called to be reconciled with one another.

Meditation: Who are the people in my life toward whom I feel anger? Pray for that person or persons now. Can the cause of the anger be resolved with justice? Can I bring myself to forgive that person? What might I do as a step toward reconciliation?

Prayer: Ever-merciful and compassionate God, you call us to oneness. With your guidance, we know that change is possible. Open our hearts to genuinely listen to others. Lead us to forgiveness, reconciliation, and peace. We ask this through your Son, our Lord Jesus Christ, who is the perfect model of forgiveness. Amen.

Pray

Readings: Deut 26:16-19; Matt 5:43-48

Scripture:
Jesus said to his disciples:
  "You have heard that it was said,
  You shall love your neighbor and hate your enemy.
But I say to you, love your enemies,
  and pray for those who persecute you,
  that you may be children of your heavenly Father."
    (Matt 5:43-45a)

Reflection: "Pray for those who persecute you." This is a challenging commandment. Sometimes, the inclusion of specific prayers for our enemies during Sunday worship can provoke feelings of outrage. How can we pray for those who have hurt us? In the aftermath of 9/11, parish communities no doubt prayed for the victims, the rescuers, the firefighters, and all of their families. How many prayed for those who had caused this suffering? Did they not also need our prayers?

Similarly, when we hear stories of children suffering as a result of sexual abuse, our hearts are moved to pray for these children and to ask God to bring healing into their lives. But, as difficult as it may be, we are also called to pray for the abusers.

A few years ago, after a colleague had repeatedly belittled my work in front of others, I lost my temper and yelled at him. Afterward, I regretted my reaction. A few days later, during the sacrament of reconciliation, a very wise priest asked me to pray for this colleague. I agreed to, not recognizing how difficult this penance would be. At that moment, I did not like this person, and I did not really want God to like him either! It took significant effort for me to find a way to genuinely pray for him.

When I finally did pray, I found my heart melting. I was able to understand him a little better, and I was able to forgive. I later apologized for yelling, and we talked about our difficulties. We continue to be good friends to this day. Prayer can bring surprising and powerful results into our lives.

Meditation: As people of prayer, we are called to love our enemies and to pray for those who persecute us. Who specifically needs my love and prayer this day? Can I genuinely lift them up in prayer?

Prayer: Ever-merciful God and Father, you have chosen us to be your children, and you call us to lives of prayer. Guide us in every aspect of our lives, and lead us toward reconciliation. We ask this through Christ our Lord. Amen.

Time Apart

Readings: Gen 15:5-12, 17-18; Phil 3:17–4:1; Luke 9:28b-36

Scripture:
Jesus took Peter, John, and James
   and went up to the mountain to pray. (Luke 9:28b)

Reflection: Those who go on retreat often compare this time apart to a mountaintop experience. Being away from the cacophony of sounds that confront us every day, away from emails, cell phones, pagers, news broadcasts, and other distractions, we have an opportunity to truly listen to God's voice. People often reach new insights in such settings, insights that help them make sense out of their lives and put issues in perspective. Priests and religious have long known the benefits of annual retreats, and more and more laypeople are discovering the advantages as well. While it can be disarming to be out of touch for a few days, some time apart to pray can be rejuvenating. Many find a similar experience of rejuvenation in the wilderness on camping trips.

As the cover of this book suggests, mountaintop experiences often arise out of the desert, when we are away from luxury and excess and can focus on essentials. This is perhaps one reason Lent can be such a powerful experience. The entire church is now in the desert of Lent, preparing ourselves for mountaintop encounters, preparing together to hear God's word in our lives more clearly. Our usual routine has been disturbed. Our church décor is muted and serene. We may find ourselves surrounded by sand or sackcloth or dry branches. Without clutter or distraction, we listen attentively.

The transfiguration scene has sometimes been compared to the post-resurrection appearances of the risen Christ. There is an other-worldly dimension as Moses and Elijah appear and the voice of God we hear: "This is my chosen Son; listen to him" (Luke 9:35). And so, buoyed up by this reminder of the glory of the Resurrection, let us be attentive.

Meditation: What could I do to create more space in my life for listening to God? How might I create an atmosphere of serenity in my life, even for just a few moments a day?

Prayer: God of beauty and light, you have spoken through the prophets and have sent us your Son. You desire to speak to us. You call us back to you. Open the ears of our hearts so that we might truly hear your word in our lives. We ask this through your Son, empowered by the Holy Spirit. Amen.

True Forgiveness

Readings: Dan 9:4b-10; Luke 6:36-38

Scripture:
Jesus said to his disciples:
   "Be merciful, just as your Father is merciful.

"Stop judging and you will not be judged.
Stop condemning and you will not be condemned.
Forgive and you will be forgiven." (Luke 6:36-37)

Reflection: Adults can learn a lot from watching children at play. The scene might go something like this: Kate picks up a toy that Jack is playing with. Jack gets upset and begins to cry in protest. At this point, an adult or an older child comes over to ask, "What's the matter?" Jack tells the story, and Kate returns the toy and says, "Sorry!" A few minutes later, the children are playing as though they're the best of friends, and all troubles are forgotten.

   As adults, we tend not to forgive quite so readily. If somebody hurts us, we remain wary that we might be hurt again. We can become cynical. No matter how sincere the apology, we may wonder if the other person really means it. Even if somebody unintentionally hurts us—whether out of carelessness or forgetfulness—and then apologizes, we may wonder whether there isn't a darker motive behind the action. It may take a long time for our trust to be restored. "Once bitten, twice shy," as the old saying goes.

We rejoice that God's forgiveness of our transgressions has no such hesitation. God loves us and welcomes us back with great joy, a model that we are called to follow.

The gospel calls on us to stop judging, stop condemning, and to begin forgiving. For this to happen, we need to hold one another in higher esteem. We need to become more trusting. We need to love as Jesus loves and see good in one another. We need to allow our hearts to melt and our relationships to heal. This is what it means to be part of the Body of Christ.

Meditation: Who are the people in my life that I have not forgiven? Is it possible that I have judged them too harshly? Can I find it in my heart to be merciful toward them? Is there good in them that I have not previously acknowledged?

Prayer: Ever-merciful God, you opened the eyes of the blind and caused them to see. Open my eyes to the times when I judge others. Show me the goodness in those who have hurt me. Teach me the path to forgiveness. Show me how to let go of past hurts and begin anew. I humbly ask this, through Christ the Lord. Amen.

Heavy Burdens

Readings: Isa 1:10, 16-20; Matt 23:1-12

Scripture:
For they preach what they do not practice.
They tie up heavy burdens hard to carry
    and lay them on people's shoulders,
    but they will not lift a finger to move them. (Matt 23:3b-4)

Reflection: Rules and regulations. Forms to be filled out in triplicate. Processes and procedures. When to stop and when to go. Quality assurance. Rules of the road. Procedures. This is how it is to be done. Instructions to follow. Deadlines. Obey.

So much of our lives is about conforming to the expectations placed on us. In order for society to function, there must be rules and regulations. There must be standards of behavior. We must be able to trust that our property will not be stolen, that our work will not be undone, that our safety will not be compromised. Our leaders must enact legislation for our protection. We stop at stop signs and proceed on green lights. There are even unwritten rules in our personal relationships. If I confide in you, you will keep my secret. If you promise to return something to me, you will. If a child promises to be home before dark, obedience is important.

Yes, our society functions based on rules and shared expectations. Sometimes, however, there can be a danger of creating rules for some but not for others, or creating rules that benefit some, but place undue burdens on others. For this, the Pharisees were criticized. They did not practice what they preached, but they expected obedience from others. The rules that they outlined were oppressive burdens.

Meditation: Jesus tells us: "My yoke is easy, and my burden light" (Matt 11:30). When we are in positions of responsibility—with family, friends, customers, students, parishioners, or coworkers—do we assess the impact and reasonableness of our expectations? In what ways are we placing undue burdens on others?

Prayer: All-knowing and ever-merciful God, you sent your Son to become one with us, to know our fatigue and our struggles. Give us wisdom, integrity, and determination to practice what we preach and to lighten the burden of others. Push us forward when we hesitate and show us the way. We ask this in the name of your Son, Jesus Christ our Lord. Amen.

Without Hesitation

Readings: Jer 18:18-20; Matt 20:17-28

Scripture:
He said to her, "What do you wish?"
She answered him,
   "Command that these two sons of mine sit,
   one at your right and the other at your left, in your
      kingdom." (Matt 20:21)

Reflection: When we hear this same story told in Mark's Gospel (see Mark 10:32-45), it is James and John themselves, the sons of Zebedee, who ask to sit at the right and left hand of Jesus in glory. In Matthew, it is their mother who makes the request. Since Matthew's Gospel is thought to have been written later than Mark's, we wonder if Matthew might have altered the story to make the disciples look better, for it is indeed audacious to make such a request.

Two thousand years later, parents are still making audacious requests for their children. Some parents try to secure special favors for their children, a practice commonly denounced as nepotism. Such requests often lead to unjust, preferential treatment; yet we wonder if, at heart, the requests might be rooted in a noble desire for one's children to succeed in life—a desire motivated by love. All loving parents want what is best for their children.

In today's Scripture passage, the mother of James and John makes her request immediately after hearing Jesus announce that he was about to be handed over to the chief priests and scribes, condemned to death, mocked, scourged, and crucified. Yet the mother believed Jesus unquestioningly when he said that he would be raised on the third day—and so she fell on her knees in homage and humbly made this startling request. She was the first to speak after Jesus' dramatic pronouncement of the fate that awaited him.

This mother was also among those loyal followers who were present at the crucifixion and who witnessed the earthquake that followed (see Matt 27:54-56). She listened, she saw, and she believed.

Meditation: In pondering the extraordinary faith of the mother of James and John, let us ask ourselves how quick we are to believe and accept the word of God. Do we believe wholeheartedly? Are we willing to act based on God's word, or do we hesitate?

Prayer: God of power and might, you have provided us with many models of extraordinary faith. Look down with favor on all parents who seek to do the best for their children. Give us the courage and the will to respond without hesitation to do what you would have us do. For this we pray. Amen.

Learning to Listen

Readings: Jer 17:5-10; Luke 16:19-31

Scripture:
Then Abraham said,
  "If they will not listen to Moses and the prophets,
  neither will they be persuaded
  if someone should rise from the dead." (Luke 16:31)

Reflection: In many parishes, adults are preparing for baptism, and this is cause for rejoicing. Catholics call this process "RCIA," or *Rite of Christian Initiation of Adults.* Anglicans and some other denominations call it the "baptismal catechumenate."

One of the cornerstones of this process is reflection on the word of God. Catechumens (those preparing for baptism) are ritually dismissed after the homily. They, together with a catechist, go off to reflect further on the gospel, while the rest of the community celebrates the Liturgy of the Eucharist. This intense reflection on the gospel is part of the apprenticeship into the Christian life. We trust that the word of God is formative, and that this attentive listening and pondering will strengthen their journey of faith. Those of us raised in the Christian faith also need to continue to grow in our ability to hear God's word, for such attentive listening is a supreme opportunity to discern God's message for our lives.

The parable in today's gospel describes the rich man and Lazarus, separated in death as in life. In life, the rich man did not even notice Lazarus at his gate. After death, Lazarus is in the bosom of Abraham, and the rich man suffers in the netherworld, yearning for a mere sip of water. The rich man was not evil. He was merely preoccupied with his wealth and did not notice the suffering of those around him. The rich man pleads with Abraham that a messenger might be sent to warn his brothers so that they do not suffer the same fate as he; but Abraham points out that Scripture already gave a warning, yet the brothers did not listen.

Jesus did rise from the dead, and we have listened. Let us continue to be attentive to the Good News.

Meditation: Do we attentively listen to the proclamation of the word of God? When we realize that Scripture is calling us to change something about our lives, do we take that seriously, or do we procrastinate or pretend not to notice? What will it take for us to listen?

Prayer: God of Abraham, Isaac, and Jacob, you send prophets into our lives to enable us to hear. Bless and protect all those who proclaim your word. Open our ears and our hearts to truly listen. Show us your message for our lives, and push us forward to respond. We ask this through your Son, and through the power of the Holy Spirit, who opens our hearts to hear. Amen.

God Is Patient

Readings: Gen 37:3-4, 12-13a, 17b-28a; Matt 21:33-43, 45-56

Scripture:
But the tenants seized the servants and one they beat,
    another they killed, and a third they stoned.
Again he sent other servants, more numerous than the
    first ones,
    but they treated them in the same way. (Matt 21:35-36)

Reflection: It is fascinating to hear the stories of how some people entered ministry. Often the experience of being called to ministry was manifest long before they responded. Their family or worship community might have noticed certain traits and encouraged them. God may have been calling them, giving them a true sense of peace when they began to respond affirmatively in the desired direction; but it may still have taken a while for them to notice or get up the courage to respond.

In our Christian life, sometimes we can be slow learners. We don't always catch on to where God is calling us. It is heartwarming to remember that God continues to call us even if we do not respond right away. If the call is genuine, God will continue to call us. This is true regardless of our vocation, whether to ordained or lay ministry, married or single life, religious life or a particular career. When we say yes to God's plan for our lives—whatever that may be and however long it may take us to wake up and say yes—at that moment, we experience true peace.

God's persistence and patience is also evident when we sin. How many of us have not felt discouraged when we notice that our examination of conscience turns up the same issues time after time? We often keep falling into the same patterns, repeating the same sins, despite knowing that we should act differently.

Just like the owner of the vineyard who continued to send servants, God continues to try to get our attention, to invite us to repent, to reform our lives, and to become the people that God wishes us to be.

Meditation: Am I following the path that God wants for my life? In what ways is God trying to get my attention? How am I being called to change?

Prayer: God of the vineyard, you have a plan for our world and for our lives. Give us the wisdom to know your will and the courage to say yes. Forgive our repeated failings and have mercy on us. We ask this through Jesus Christ our Lord. Amen.

Unconditional Love and Mercy

Readings: Mic 7:14-15, 18-20; Luke 15:1-3, 11-32

Scripture:
So he got up and went back to his father.
While he was still a long way off,
   his father caught sight of him, and was filled with
      compassion.
He ran to his son, embraced him and kissed him.
   (Luke 15:20)

Reflection: Today's gospel tells the Parable of the Prodigal Son. The story could also be called the Parable of the Compassionate and Merciful Father.

   At times in our lives, we act like the younger son. We have indeed been given many blessings. God has endowed us with the gifts of patience and friendship, love and warmth, good health and family, time and wisdom, among many others. We have put some of those gifts to good use, helping others and becoming the people that God calls us to be; but we have squandered other gifts, wasting time on frivolous pursuits or making unwise choices. We may have hurt our friends or neglected to act as we know we should. We do not always show gratitude for the gifts we are given. But at some point, we do recognize our error and we begin to return home. This recognition and desire for reconciliation are indeed cause for rejoicing, as the father in today's parable demonstrated.

At times in our lives, we will be called to be like that father. We will be the ones who unreservedly welcome back the one who has gone astray, who forgive wholeheartedly and rejoice at the restored relationship. This is indeed the vision that God has for us. We can imagine God rejoicing with exuberance whenever one of us recognizes our waywardness and begins to journey home—and so we are called to model that mercy and compassion in our relationships with others.

Meditation: In what ways have I misused the gifts that God has given me? With whom do I need to reconcile? To whom do I need to show greater compassion?

Prayer: God of mercy, your gift of forgiveness is hard for us to fathom. You model the utmost love and kindness, and you accept the plea of the sinner without hesitation. Enable us to be compassionate and merciful. Show us how to most effectively use the gifts you give us. Soften any anger in our hearts and allow us to love and forgive unconditionally. We ask this through Jesus, the ultimate model of love and compassion. Amen.

A Second Chance at Life

Readings: Exod 3:1-8a, 13-15; 1 Cor 10:1-6, 10-12; Luke 13:1-9

Scripture:
There once was a person who had a fig tree planted in
    his orchard,
  and when he came in search of fruit on it but found none,
  he said to the gardener,
    "For three years now I have come in search of fruit on
      this fig tree
  but have found none. So cut it down.
  Why should it exhaust the soil?"
He said to him in reply,
    "Sir, leave it for this year also,
  and I shall cultivate the ground around it and fertilize it;
  it may bear fruit in the future.
If not you can cut it down." (Luke 13:6-9)

Reflection: Because of the gardener's plea, the fig tree was
given one more year to bear fruit. Whenever we hear this
story, we may imagine ourselves as that tree and ask whether
our lives are bearing fruit. Jesus tells us that we bear much
fruit when we abide in him (see John 15:5). When we are
centered in Christ, we are able to let go of all that hinders us
and are able to wholeheartedly do God's will. Am I centered

in Christ? Are sin, bitterness, self-centeredness, or other issues preventing me from embracing God's will?

There is an urgency in this passage; the time remaining is limited and we must not delay. When people experience a brush with death or learn that they have a fatal illness, they experience a similar urgency—and often use this opportunity to reform their lives, to make amends with those they have hurt, and to more genuinely appreciate the gifts God has given them.

We often hear that we should live every day as if it were our last. The urgency in this message may scare us, but we are not alone on this journey. Jesus is the vine and we are the branches (see John 15:5). Do I recognize my connectedness to Christ? Does my life reflect this connection? If yes, I will be able to repeat the words of Jesus without hesitation: "Father, into your hands I commend my spirit" (Luke 23:46).

Meditation: Is this the year that Christ is calling me to abide in him and produce good fruit, like the fig tree that was given a second chance? How could my life more clearly reflect my connectedness to Christ? What type of cultivation will help me to grow?

Prayer: God of mercy and compassion, open the eyes of our hearts to recognize the fruit that you wish us to produce. Give us the cultivation we need to become the people you wish us to be. We ask this through your Son and our Lord, Jesus Christ. Amen.

No Limits

Readings: 2 Kgs 5:1-15ab; Luke 4:24-30

Scripture:
It was to none of these that Elijah was sent,
  but only to a widow in Zarephath in the land of Sidon.
    (Luke 4:26)

Reflection: As members of various communities, we gain a certain sense of belonging and comfort. Employees express pride in the company where they work. Students take delight in the reputation of their school. Parish feast days honor all those who have worshiped in that community in the past—and, at the same time, celebrate what God continues to do for the community. During the Olympics, our national pride shines forth as we rejoice in the accomplishments of our country's athletes (even if we had never heard their names before that competition).

One danger with such bonds, however, is that they can exclude. When a group of friends roots for a hockey team in the company of a fan of the other team, tensions can rise. When we are not part of a certain clique, we can feel left out. In addition to excluding others, our dedication to a group might also cause us to be more hesitant in how we speak or act, sometimes to the point of going along with a group rather than doing what is right. Even with these two risks associated with belonging, communities are vital to our well-being and sense of identity.

In today's gospel, Luke emphasizes the themes of inclusiveness and universality—and Jesus' words demonstrate that he does not hesitate to speak contrary to the expectations of his community, a community that believed God's salvation was offered to only a small group. Jesus says the message of God's salvation is greater than this. The Good News is not announced only to Jewish people. It is not announced only to religious leaders. It is not announced only to men. The Good News is a message for all.

Here, by pointing back to a story about Elijah, Jesus is reminding his listeners that this universality is really not new. Even in the days of prophet Elijah, God's message was proclaimed to those outside of Israel. God's love is boundless.

Meditation: Do we sometimes fail to recognize that God's grace is too vast to be contained? Are our communities welcoming to all? What barriers exist? Does it make us uncomfortable to realize that God loves even those whom we dislike? When have I seen God's love overcoming barriers?

Prayer: Creator God, your love surpasses all limits. Wherever there is misunderstanding or division, in our families, in our communities, and in the church, bring healing. We ask this through Christ our Lord. Amen.

Forgiveness

Readings: Dan 3:25, 34-43; Matt 18:21-35

Scripture:
Peter approached Jesus and asked him,
  "Lord, if my brother sins against me,
  how often must I forgive him?
As many as seven times?"
Jesus answered, "I say to you, not seven times but seventy-
    seven times." (Matt 18:21-22)

Reflection: Anne's assignment was to plan a big event for
her company. Since the company did not pay its employees
for overtime, Anne suggested to her manager Bill that the
scope of the event be scaled back so that the planning would
fit within her working hours. Bill was alarmed at her sug-
gestion and asked Anne to do all that was envisioned. He
told her to keep track of her hours and promised to arrange
for Anne to take time off with pay after the event.

  This seemed fair, so Anne proceeded to work many long
hours, and the event was a big success. Afterward, Anne
really needed a chance to rest and requested some days off
with pay. Bill seemed puzzled. He had no recollection of
their earlier conversation and told her that time off in lieu
of overtime was against company policy. Anne felt betrayed
and used.

When promises are broken and injustices occur, bitterness, resentment, and anger can build inside us. Sometimes we bury such feelings rather than acknowledge them. But at some point we need to explicitly decide to forgive and to let go of the past in order to move forward and embrace the future. This can be very difficult. We may need to pray fervently that God give us the grace to forgive and move on. It may be helpful for Anne to try to pray for Bill, just as Jesus commanded us to pray for those who persecute us (see Matt 5:44). When we pray for another person, we can begin to understand their weaknesses—and are able to let go of our own pain. Thus, it is for our own good and for the good of others that we follow Jesus' commandment to forgive unconditionally.

Meditation: Moving on can be very freeing. Do I hold onto past hurts and allow them to fester inside me, or do I let them go? Does somebody need to hear that I have forgiven them? Do I truly believe and accept that God has forgiven me, or do I continue to fret over past events?

Prayer: God of mercy, you provide in Jesus the model of true forgiveness. Give me the strength to be a forgiving person. Give me the confidence and assurance to know in my heart that you have indeed forgiven my sins. Allow me to forgive myself and to move on from past hurts. For this I ask, in Jesus' name. Amen.

Teaching Our Faith

Readings: Deut 4:1, 5-9; Matt 5:17-19

Scripture:
But whoever obeys and teaches these commandments
will be called greatest in the Kingdom of heaven. (Matt
5:19b)

Reflection: Christianity is not a religion for individuals. We
come to Christ in the context of a community. Members of
our families or of our parish introduce us to the word of God.
It takes meaning in our lives in part because of the value
placed on it by those we trust. We learn to interpret God's
word through the lens of the Christian tradition, and we
come to understand its message for our own lives. Young
children watch their parents singing hymns and they learn
to praise God. Our obligations toward one another continue
throughout our lives.

The communal nature of our faith is important in light of
today's gospel, for we see that it is not enough to obey the
commandments. We must also teach the commandments to
others.

St. Francis of Assisi once taught that we should preach the
gospel always and, when necessary, use words. We can teach
much about the commandments through our actions,
through the ways that we lead our lives. The commandments

have already been etched on our hearts (see Jer 31:33; Rom 2:15). When we reflect outwardly what we already bear within, we become role models for those around us.

Whenever we plead for fairness and justice—when we challenge big corporations that do not honor their commitments, when we encourage children to play by the rules, when we draw attention to corrupt practices, when we organize parish initiatives to address issues of injustice, when we stand up for the underdog, when we act with justice and mercy—each and every one of these actions shows a commitment to teaching the commandments.

If we teach others, we also encourage them with our support and rejoice with them. Let us delight whenever we witness others growing in faith.

Meditation: In what ways am I teaching and respecting the commandments? In what ways do I model my faith to others?

Prayer: God of compassion, You gave us the commandments out of your love for us. Give us wisdom to follow your precepts. Give us the strength and courage to lead others. We ask this through Christ our Lord. Amen.

Prophets

Readings: Jer 7:23-28; Luke 11:14-23

Scripture:
From the day that your fathers left the land of Egypt even
    to this day,
  I have sent you untiringly all my servants the prophets.
    (Jer 7:25)

Reflection: In today's world, we are bombarded with information. We have around-the-clock news coverage that tells us of violence, warfare, political events, weather disasters—and the occasional good news—in every corner of the world.

Amid so much information, it can be hard for us to identify that which is really important and relevant for us. Of all the events going on in the world, which should we care about? When natural disasters strike in distant lands, should we respond? If so, how? Many worthwhile humanitarian organizations encourage us to open our wallets and step up to help others who are in need. Some of these organizations and people function as modern-day prophets, appealing to our sense of goodwill and calling us to do what is right.

It is encouraging to be reminded that God continues to send prophets to enlighten us. Who are these prophets in our world today? Are they pastors and bishops, who draw our attention to social justice issues in our communities and call us to more heartfelt prayer and action? Are they lobbyists, who draw our attention to issues and people that governments are neglecting? Maybe the prophets are those who pay for advertisements that remind us not to drink and drive. Or perhaps the prophets are those who remind us that saving money is not a good enough reason to illegally copy music or computer software. Similarly, when parents encourage their children to behave responsibly, perhaps they are prophets sent by God to fulfill just such a function.

At our baptism, we were each anointed with chrism as a reminder that we participate with Christ as priest, prophet, and king. We are all called by God to serve as prophets, to bring the information of God's love to others in word and deed.

Meditation: To whom do I listen? Am I seeking to discern and follow God's will as I sort out all the voices I hear? Do I listen with an open heart? How am I living out my baptismal call to be a prophet in Christ? Rejoice and thank God for the prophets in your life.

Prayer: God of heaven and earth, bless and strengthen all whom you send as prophets. Lift me up and guide me; give me the words to speak. Push me forward when I hesitate. Open my ears to hear the messages you want me to hear. I ask this through Christ, my Lord and my Savior, in the power of the Holy Spirit. Amen.

March 16: Friday of the Third Week of Lent

Wholehearted Love

Readings: Hos 14:2-10; Mark 12:28-34

Scripture:
You shall love the Lord your God with all your heart,
 with all your soul,
 with all your mind,
 and with all your strength. (Mark 12:30)

Reflection: Driving instructors emphasize the danger of distractions. Eating, drinking, changing CDs, talking on a cell phone, or reading a map can all be dangerous because they take our attention away from what is truly essential: watching where we are going. Sometimes, even when we think we are being attentive, we can be momentarily distracted by an accident at the side of the road, a sign advertising a big sale, or even a cute dog. Suddenly, we might hear the toot of a horn behind us and realize we are waiting at a green light.

If we struggle to remain focused on something as commonplace as driving, perhaps it is not surprising that we sometimes struggle to remain focused on our faith life. In today's gospel, Jesus gives us a point of focus and calls us to respond to God with our whole being. How do we love God wholeheartedly and unreservedly? Fortunately, the initiative comes from God, not from us. We were created to love God. The Holy Spirit dwells within us and creates within us a yearning for oneness with our Creator. It is therefore easier for us to love God and to say yes to God than it is for us to turn away. Pope Benedict XVI writes in his encyclical, *Deus Caritas Est*, "Since God has first loved us (cf. 1 Jn 4:10), love is now no longer a mere 'command'; it is the response to the gift of love with which God draws near to us."

Sometimes we may not act as though we love God. We may not take time to pray. We might treat other aspects of our lives as though they are more important than God and allow them to dominate our lives. For example, we might devote ourselves so unreservedly to our work or our hobbies that we lose our sense of priorities. In the process, we might neglect the people in our lives who matter most to us. We might become boastful of our accomplishments, forgetting that thanks and praise are due to God for the very ability to participate in those activities. Sometimes we may even choose to disregard where God is calling us. But we take comfort in knowing that God will continue to call us. That invitation is always there. Even when we turn away, God continues to love us and welcome us back.

Meditation: What activities consume too much of my attention? What interferes with my relationship with God? How could I respond more wholeheartedly to God's love?

Prayer: Loving and tender God, you ask us to love you wholeheartedly. Open our eyes to recognize those aspects of our life that impede our unreserved response. Enable us to be loving people, caring for all who are in need. We ask this through Christ our Lord. Amen.

Humbling Ourselves

Readings: Hos 6:1-6; Luke 18:9-14

Scripture:
I tell you, the latter went home justified, not the former;
   for everyone who exalts himself will be humbled,
   and the one who humbles himself will be exalted.
      (Luke 18:14)

Reflection: Jane, the retreat director, had a reputation for her rather eccentric methods, but she had certainly led this group of college students to valuable insights about the gospel message. She caught them by surprise with important life lessons at every turn. It had been a week of growth.

As the first few students enthusiastically entered the hall for the big banquet, they saw that there were two very comfortable armchairs and several metal folding chairs at each table. With a laugh, Sally and her friends raced for the more comfy armchairs. Those who came later had to make do with the cold metal chairs.

After everybody was seated, Jane made a few announcements. First, she hoped that those in the armchairs were enjoying their comfort. Sally looked at her friends and smiled—these chairs were nice! Sally's smile disappeared as Jane went on to ask that those sitting in the armchairs remain seated until all the others had finished eating. She asked them to place their wrists against the chair arms and to not move them for any reason until given permission. Sally didn't like this! With her wrists on the chair arms, she couldn't even reach her glass of water. But that wasn't all! Jane went on to say that they must smile in silence throughout the meal, so that the others could enjoy their meals without hearing any whining! Only after the dessert had been served were those in the armchairs finally permitted to speak and invited to approach the banquet table.

Surrounded by the smell of good food, watching the others eat, listening in silence to their conversation and trying to ignore her own hunger, Sally had plenty of time to reflect on her behavior. Why did she always want the place of honor? Why did she always take the most comfortable option? Maybe others needed the sturdy back support and comfort of these chairs more than she did. It had not even occurred to her to take a lesser place at the table or to really think about the comfort of others. It would next time.

Meditation: In what aspects of my life could I take the lesser place at table? In what big or small ways am I being called to sacrifice for the good of others?

Prayer: God of infinite love, lead me to be more generous and self-giving. Give me the grace to be more aware and considerate of the needs of others. Bless and strengthen all who seek to follow you. For this I earnestly pray, in a spirit of humility. Amen.

Gratitude

Readings: Josh 5:9a, 10-12; 2 Cor 5:17-21; Luke 15:1-3, 11-32

Scripture:
He said to his father in reply,
"Look, all these years I served you
and not once did I disobey your orders;
yet you never gave me even a young goat to feast on
with my friends." (Luke 15:29)

Reflection: Our society is founded on basic principles of justice and fair play. Unions press employers for equitable treatment based on merit and seniority. Scholarship committees strive to give money to the most deserving students. We expect that those who work hard will be rewarded for their efforts and that those who break the rules will be punished.

And yet, real life experience shows us that such rules of equity and justice do not always apply. Sometimes bad things happen to good people. And sometimes, as in today's gospel, good things happen to people who may not deserve them.

The younger son in this parable has behaved truly despicably. Motivated by greed, he callously asked his father for his share of his inheritance immediately, rather than waiting for the death of his father. Who among us would expect our parents to sell their property and give us half their retirement savings now? Not only did this son act audaciously in his request, he then went off and squandered the money on a life of debauchery. He was not a good person. He did not deserve to be forgiven, and he certainly did not deserve to have a lavish feast in his honor. And yet, the father reacted with joy at his son's return.

From the point of view of the elder brother, this treatment is unjust and illogical. The way that he expresses his outrage speaks volumes, though. His words to his father sound like the words of a hired hand, serving his father and obeying. The older son expected equitable treatment as one would associate with a contract. Yet his father's love, and God's love for us, is not based on a contract. It is a gift given freely and without limit.

Meditation: Do I ever feel resentful toward those who seem to get ahead with little effort, or those who get more than they deserve? Do I approach God as though in a contractual relationship, doing my duty and expecting blessings in return? Or do I approach God as a loving child, eager to please a doting parent and ready to express joy at any and every blessing that comes my way?

Prayer: God of boundless love, you shower many blessings on your people. Create in us an attitude of gratitude, not entitlement. May we rejoice in your blessings in our lives and in the lives of others. With grateful hearts, we pray. Amen.

March 19: Saint Joseph,
Husband of the Blessed Virgin Mary

A New Outlook

Readings: 2 Sam 7:4-5a, 12-14a, 16; Rom 4:13, 16-18, 22; Luke 2:41-51a (second option)

Scripture:
When his parents saw him,
  they were astonished,
  and his mother said to him,
  "Son, why have you done this to us?
Your father and I have been looking for you with great
  anxiety." (Luke 2:48)

Reflection: In this rare glimpse of Jesus' childhood, today's gospel recounts the story of Jesus, Mary, and Joseph making their annual pilgrimage to Jerusalem for the Feast of Passover. On the way home to Nazareth, Mary and Joseph realize that Jesus is not with them, and they frantically search for three days before finding him in the Temple, sitting in the midst of the teachers, astounding all with his level of knowledge and comprehension of Scripture.

In Luke's Gospel, this episode marks the transition from Jesus' childhood to his adult ministry, the first visible sign that he was not like other children. He was already on his mission, a mission that would end in suffering, death, and resurrection. We are given a privileged glimpse of Mary and

Joseph and their reaction. They were coming to learn more about who Jesus was, and their outlook was being challenged and changed as a result.

Like Mary and Joseph, all who participate in any part of Jesus' journey experience some surprises. This happened to the disciples, and we see their bewilderment as they witnessed the suffering and death of their Messiah. Bewilderment and awe were also part of the resurrection experiences, and they continue to be part of our experiences as Christians. The more we come to know Christ, the more we see the world through new eyes. All who follow Christ gain far more than they ever dreamed possible—and never cease to be amazed. As we grow ever closer to Christ and as our understanding deepens, our perspective is changed. We become more appreciative of the beauty in God's creation and in each person that we meet.

Meditation: In what ways does my Christian faith continue to challenge and shape my outlook? In what ways does Jesus continue to surprise me in my own life?

Prayer: Father in heaven, thank you for the witness of Mary and Joseph as they came to grasp more deeply the nature of Jesus' mission. Guide us also to see with new eyes and to deepen our awareness of Jesus' presence in our lives. We ask this in Jesus' name, through the intercession of Mary and Joseph. Amen.

Becoming Whole

Readings: Ezek 47:1-9, 12; John 5:1-16

Scripture:
After this Jesus found him in the temple area and said
  to him,
  "Look, you are well; do not sin any more,
  so that nothing worse may happen to you." (John 5:14)

Reflection: Throughout John's Gospel, water has significant
meaning. We recall the miracle at Cana, Jesus' baptism by
John in the Jordan, and Jesus' discussion with the Samaritan
woman about living water. We know the impact of baptism
in our own lives. So when we hear that Jesus is approaching
a man near a pool where people come for healing, we an-
ticipate something dramatic.

Jesus asks the man if he desires to be well. Such a question
might seem outlandish—who would not want to be well?
This man had been ill for thirty-eight years. But in this in-
stance, some suggest, Jesus is asking about more than physical healing. He is asking about wellness or wholeness, which
may suggest forgiveness of sins, overcoming of character
weaknesses, or growth to one's full potential. After the healing, when Jesus encounters him in the Temple, Jesus declares
that the man is indeed well. Later, the man reports to the

Jewish authorities that Jesus had made him well. He has become a proclaimer of the Good News.

The mention of sin in this passage is a surprise to the reader; it is the first occurrence in John's Gospel since John the Baptist declared Jesus to be the Lamb of God who takes away the sin of the world (see John 1:29). In Jesus' instructions to this man, exhorting him to sin no more, Jesus is drawing attention to the seriousness of sinning after having been made whole. Just as the early church struggled over how to deal with those who denied their faith after baptism, Jesus is drawing attention to the potentially serious consequences of sin. This is a caution to us all.

Meditation: Jesus raises a poignant question. How would I answer? Am I ready and willing to accept Jesus' invitation to be made whole? In what aspects of my life am I not whole? In what ways am I in need of healing, forgiveness, and transformation?

Prayer: God of healing and mercy, you sent your Son to redeem, heal, and forgive humanity and to bring us back to you. As we continue our Lenten journey toward the great feast of Easter, make us whole. Forgive our sins. Transform our hearts. Renew us. Give us strength to proclaim your good news through word and deed. We ask this through Christ, who makes all things new. Amen.

The Will of God

Readings: Isa 49:8-15; John 5:17-30

Scripture:
I cannot do anything on my own;
   I judge as I hear, and my judgment is just,
   because I do not seek my own will
   but the will of the one who sent me. (John 5:30)

Reflection: I have a wooden plaque on an end table in my living room with the words: "I have all the time I need to do all that God intends me to do this day." I take great comfort in that motto. Sometimes life feels overwhelming, and we realize that it is impossible to accomplish all that we are being asked to do. It is humanly impossible to balance everything. Humanly impossible. But if it is God's will, anything is possible.

Of course, the wooden plaque may also be reminding me that some prioritization is needed among the tasks before me, for God does not expect me to complete everything. Some things will need to be deferred to another day, or I will need to ask others to share the load if everything really does need to be accomplished.

Another way of reading the plaque would be as a form of gentle prodding. Maybe I really do have the time I need to accomplish all that God expects me to do this day, but maybe

I need to use my time more wisely and set aside things that might be my will and not God's will. Or maybe I need to revisit my tendency to work long hours. Maybe God is calling me to find more balance in my life, to make more time for sacred leisure.

One effect of reflecting on this motto is that I am reminded that it is ultimately God's will that matters. In today's gospel, Jesus states, "I cannot do anything on my own" and "I do not seek my own will." Let us all seek to follow Jesus' example of total attentiveness to God the Father. May we all accomplish the tasks set before us with diligence and balance in our lives.

Meditation: Do I entrust the day-to-day moments of my life to God and seek to do God's will, or do I get so caught up with trying to achieve the next deadline that I fail to notice where God might truly be calling me? Do I make enough room for God in my life?

Prayer: God of infinite wisdom, be with us in the day-to-day decisions and challenges of our lives. Push us forward when we are feeling distracted, lazy, or discouraged. Open our eyes to see opportunities for rest, balance, or needs of greater importance. May we always seek to do your will. We ask this through Jesus our Savior and Lord, and through the Holy Spirit, who gives us strength each day. Amen.

Open Hearts

Readings: Exod 32:7-14; John 5:31-47

Scripture:
You search the Scriptures,
  because you think you have eternal life through them;
  even they testify on my behalf.
But you do not come to me to have life. (John 5:39-40)

Reflection: Pharmaceutical research would be discounted as unreliable hearsay if researchers were selective about the data they examine. When researchers conduct a trial, if they record only the results of those who benefit from a drug and somehow forget to write down the results of those who show no improvement or who are harmed by a drug, the published results will be meaningless. Scientific research tries hard to eliminate such bias and to make conclusions based solely on the results obtained.

It would be nearly impossible for us to approach Scripture in such a purely scientific way because we each read Scripture through the lens of our own life experience. While we bring our own biases based on life's experiences to Scripture, we must avoid the bias that comes from searching for those parts of the Bible that we like—and discarding those parts that we do not like. Our reading then becomes as biased as the tainted research mentioned above. And we miss something important.

In today's gospel, Jesus speaks of how the Old Testament points the way to his coming. Scripture points the way for us as well. It is the ultimate tool to aid our prayer, to teach us salvation history, and to enable us to grow in our awareness of God's message in our lives today. Whenever we approach Scripture, whether in personal prayer or during common worship, we must approach it with an open heart if we are to hear what God is saying to us. If we read Scripture with an open, discerning heart, we will likewise be led to a greater recognition of the identity of Jesus. God will speak to our heart and the Holy Spirit will guide our understanding, revealing Christ's presence and drawing us into deeper communion. Great discoveries are possible.

Meditation: Lent is a time for conversion, a time when those entering the church experience their final preparations for baptism, a time when all of us are called to reflect on and to be open to God's word. How is God calling me to grow this Lent? If I take the time to prayerfully read the Bible or to listen attentively during Eucharist, what is God saying to me?

Prayer: Mighty and tender God, you call us to conversion of heart. Allow us to hear your word and to be changed by your word. We ask this through your Son and our Lord, Jesus Christ, and through the power of the Holy Spirit, who dwells in our hearts. Amen.

Accepting Feedback

Readings: Wis 2:1a, 12-22; John 7:1-2, 10, 25-30

Scripture:
Let us beset the just one, because he is obnoxious to us;
  he sets himself against our doings,
Reproaches us for transgressions of the law
  and charges us with violations of our training. (Wis 2:12)

Reflection: Annually, or perhaps semiannually, many managers sit down with their staff for individual performance reviews. These meetings can be a wonderful opportunity to hear what people really think about their work assignments and to learn about their hopes and concerns. In such meetings, managers name the strengths and weaknesses of their employee's work and are expected to identify at least one area where improvement is needed. It is this latter part that I often struggled with when I was a manager, especially for particularly strong employees. When evaluating these employees, it is easy to praise the quality, quantity, and creativity of their work, the way that they take time to help others, the way that they show leadership and suggest ways that the department could become more efficient. It can be a struggle to name areas for improvement. And yet we all know that we are imperfect and there are always aspects of our work or our lives that could be improved.

Even in such environments, where everybody knows that the manager is expected to name some areas for development, the weaknesses need to be spoken with great care. People easily become defensive and resistant to correction, and may even become antagonistic toward the one giving the feedback. While we may appreciate helpful insights, suggestions, and recommendations from close friends, hearing the exact same feedback from a stranger or a supervisor may lead to resistance. Our pride is easily hurt, even when we recognize the truth.

Perhaps that is why the people in today's first reading reacted so negatively against "the just one," the one who "reproaches us for transgressions of the law." They plotted to put him to the test, and to condemn him to a shameful death, clearly foreshadowing the fate of Jesus.

Meditation: How do we react when others question our lifestyle, our priorities, or our behavior? Do we snap at others when they correct us? Do we become defensive, or are we willing to acknowledge our weaknesses? What areas for improvement might others identify in the way I lead my life?

Prayer: God of light, you sent Jesus to be the light of the world, to convey a new vision. When my vision becomes clouded, or when the way I lead my life does not reflect your love, grant me the humility to be open to correction. Amen.

March 24: Saturday of the Fourth Week of Lent

Nicodemus

Readings: Jer 11:18-20; John 7:40-53

Scripture:
Nicodemus, one of their members who had come to him
    earlier, said to them,
  "Does our law condemn a man before it first hears him
  and finds out what he is doing?" (John 7:50-51)

Reflection: Nicodemus is an intriguing, ambiguous figure
in John's Gospel. A Pharisaic Jew, he seems sympathetic to
Jesus, but cannot quite be considered one of Jesus' followers.
In today's gospel, Nicodemus comes to Jesus' defense, but
for reasons that are rather superficial, arguing a mere tech-
nicality of the law. He does not rule out condemning Jesus
after giving him a chance to speak.

Earlier, Nicodemus acknowledged Jesus as a teacher come
from God, but something about his answer was unsatisfac-
tory to Jesus, who tried to explain to him the concept of being
born from above (see John 3:1-21). After Jesus' crucifixion,
Nicodemus accompanies Joseph of Arimathea to prepare
Jesus' body for burial (see John 19:38-42). Nicodemus brings
an enormous quantity of burial spices. Scripture scholars
debate the significance of this. Perhaps Nicodemus sees Jesus
as a great human being, worthy of love and care, so he wishes
to go to extraordinary means to preserve his body; or per-

haps the large quantity points to a total lack of belief in Jesus' pending resurrection.

In all three of these episodes, Nicodemus seems like a marginal character, one who is sympathetic to Jesus, yet one who does not quite grasp Jesus' identity. He is open and seeks to follow Jesus, and he has other praiseworthy qualities, but he falls short of fully understanding. He is trying, but his commitment seems to be lacking.

The good news for us is that God is using Nicodemus, despite his incomplete understanding. Nicodemus furthers the kingdom of God and allows Jesus to be heard.

Meditation: Am I like Nicodemus, remaining on the margins in my acknowledgment of Christ? Am I sympathetic to the Christian message without quite surrendering my previous philosophy of life? In what ways do I still need to grow to become an unreserved follower of Christ? How is God using me?

Prayer: O God of wisdom, you are all-powerful and all-knowing. I believe in you and I want to follow you. I yearn to know you. Wherever there is doubt or uncertainty in my life, guide me to a more wholehearted acceptance of you. I ask this through Christ your Son, in the power of the Holy Spirit. Amen.

A New Law

Readings: Isa 43:16-21; Phil 3:8-14; John 8:1-11

Scripture:
Jesus bent down and began to write on the ground with
    his finger.
But when they continued asking him,
   he straightened up and said to them,
    "Let the one among you who is without sin
    be the first to throw a stone at her." (John 8:6b-7)

Reflection: We all enjoy seeing the underdog emerge victo-
rious. Today's gospel story of the adulterous woman illus-
trates such a dramatic reversal of power. The scribes and
Pharisees begin by appearing strong and the woman appears
weak—but ultimately, Jesus demonstrates that the reverse
is really true.

Witnesses report having caught a woman in the act of
committing adultery, but the case they present is full of holes,
with many unanswered questions. For example, if the act
occurred in private, how did they see? Were they peeping?
If the act occurred in a brothel, why were the witnesses there?
Why was the man not also arrested? The weakness of the
case is compounded by the inability of the Pharisees and
scribes to act. Mosaic law teaches that they are to use the
death penalty for adultery; but during the time of Jesus,

Jewish people could not execute anyone because the Roman authorities had taken that right away. Only the Romans could impose the death penalty.

So the scribes and Pharisees come before Jesus powerless; and yet the accused woman shows strength. There may be parallels between her silence in the face of accusation and Jesus' silence at his trial. For Jesus, his silence would suggest character, strength, and faith in God. Perhaps the same is true of the woman, who apparently does not beg for mercy or reprieve or make any effort to defend herself. Perhaps she recognizes Jesus as the Son of God.

As Mary proclaims so eloquently in the Magnificat (see Luke 1:52), power structures are reversed in the kingdom of God. Whenever we stand accused and whenever we stand ready to accuse, may we gain strength from recalling Jesus' demonstration of mercy.

Meditation: Do I use power appropriately? Am I willing to challenge the unjust use of power in my community? What sin in my life should I acknowledge and address? Am I too quick to condemn others?

Prayer: God of wisdom, you gently but steadily nudge us to recognize our failings. Forgive our sins. Strengthen us in our pursuit of holiness. In Jesus' name we pray. Amen.

Words to Treasure

Readings: Isa 7:10-14; 8:10; Heb 10:4-10; Luke 1:26-38

Scripture:
And behold, Elizabeth, your relative,
  has also conceived a son in her old age,
  and this is the sixth month for her who was called barren;
  for nothing will be impossible for God. (Luke 1:36-37)

Reflection: "Nothing will be impossible for God." Words to treasure! Words to remember!

We often have dreams in life, dreams that may seem totally unrealistic. We might dream of what we would do if we won the lottery—of the fun we would have traveling, sailing on our new yacht, or maybe enjoying a beautiful mansion overlooking a lake. Young children may dream about what they want to be when they grow up. Adults might dream of the future happiness that they desire for their children or students. We might imagine and hope that our parish community will grow over time. We might dream of what the world would be like if we could eradicate HIV/AIDS, poverty, drug abuse, violence, and criminal activity.

"Nothing will be impossible for God." Mary undoubtedly already knew that God was capable of awesome miracles. She knew that both Sarah and Hannah, though barren and aged, had given birth; and she had just heard the angel Gabriel say that through the power of God this same miracle was now being repeated with Elizabeth.

Every time we gather for Eucharist, we too are reminded of the power of God and gain a glimpse of the future that we will experience when Christ comes again. Healing, peace, and eternal life are all part of that picture, part of the dream that is more than a dream. It is a promise. Just as God promises Mary that she will bear a son, God promises us new life in Christ.

Mary demonstrated courage and trust when she responded, "May it be done to me according to your word" (Luke 1:38). Like Mary, let us also show courage and trust in accepting our part of God's plan. Let us push ourselves to get past all the things that might get in our way—our insecurities, hesitations, shyness, doubts, preoccupations—and let us allow our lives to be shaped by God's dream for us. Let us allow ourselves to be surprised.

Meditation: What hampers me from seeing and accepting God's plan for my life? In what ways have I already said yes to God's plan? If I ponder the words, "nothing will be impossible for God," in what aspects of my life does this give me hope?

Prayer: Mary, you provide us with a model of courage and trust. May we also be women and men of courage. May we also find the strength to say yes to God. May we also find delight and wonder beyond our imagination. May we, like you, be full of grace and may the Lord be with us. Amen.

God Is Present

Readings: Num 21:4-9; John 8:21-30

Scripture:
So Moses prayed for the people, and the LORD said to
    Moses,
    "Make a saraph and mount it on a pole,
    and whoever looks at it after being bitten will live."
        (Num 21:7b-8)

Reflection: In this reading, the people had lost patience with
Moses and with God. They had been wandering in the desert
for a long time and were disheartened. Their faith was weak.
They complained bitterly. After encountering saraph serpents,
they recognized their sin and repented. They apologized to
Moses and pleaded with him to intercede for them before
God. In response to that prayer, God directed Moses to place
a bronze serpent on a pole. From that time on, anybody bitten
by a serpent could look at the bronze serpent and live.

  We too can become disheartened, and sometimes we need
something tangible or visible to comfort us and remind us
that God has not forgotten us. There is a story of a young child
who was afraid of the dark and did not want to go to bed
alone. She refused to go to bed unless somebody sat beside
her while she fell asleep. Her mother assured her that she was

not alone, that God was with her. The young child replied that she did not want God; she wanted someone with skin.

We have a God with skin. Ever since the incarnation of Christ, God has been tangibly present in our world. We see Jesus in the face of others. When a friend dries our tears or comforts us, God is there. We hear God's word proclaimed. The sick experience God's healing touch when anointed. At baptisms, confirmations, and ordinations, we sense the outpouring of the Holy Spirit as the sweet smell of sacred chrism permeates the air. In the Eucharist, not only do we see and touch the presence of Christ, but we also taste it. God is present to all our senses.

God meets us where we are and provides us with what we need to be comforted. And Jesus is the greatest tangible evidence that God has not forgotten us, that God cares for us more than we could ever imagine.

Meditation: In what ways am I reminded of God's presence this day? Who or what conveys God's love to me?

Prayer: Loving and attentive God, comfort me and let me be sure of your presence. Be with me whenever I feel isolated or alone. May I be a source of comfort to others. Bless all those who are alone and in need of support with the presence and compassion of others. Amen.

Being True to Oneself

Readings: Dan 3:14-20, 91-92, 95; John 8:31-42

Scripture:
They answered and said to him, "Our father is Abraham."
Jesus said to them, "If you were Abraham's children,
   you would be doing the works of Abraham.
But now you are trying to kill me,
   a man who has told you the truth that I heard from God;
   Abraham did not do this." (John 8:39-40)

Reflection: The Christian message continually calls us to authenticity and truth. We must be true to ourselves and not claim to be something we are not. This is part of the reason that Jesus chastises the Jewish leaders in today's gospel. Jesus is speaking as a heavenly messenger, one sent by God, and yet "Abraham's children" seek to kill him. This attitude undermines their claim that Abraham is their true father, since Abraham was known for the hospitality he showed to heavenly messengers.

In Genesis 18, angels visit Abraham and Sarah. The passage at times refers to one messenger and at times to three messengers, so some church fathers took this as a veiled early reference to the triune God, the Holy Trinity, three-in-one. Andrei Rublev picked up this ancient theme and made it come alive in his fifteenth-century icon of the Holy Trinity.

In the icon, the three figures are oriented toward each other. In their midst stands a chalice, a eucharistic symbol, the cup of salvation. When we gaze at the icon, we are drawn into the inner circle. The perfect symmetry of the artwork creates a sense of peace. Our true home is within this divine inner circle, this house of love, at peace and in harmony.

The gospel calls us over and over again to consistency and harmony. We must live what we believe and not give in to peer pressure or try to be someone we're not. Doing God's will leads to a deep sense of peace, and this peace confirms our true vocation. If we have chosen well, in big or small choices in our lives, we will experience the peace that the world cannot give, the peace that comes from knowing deep in our hearts that we are doing God's will, the peace that Abraham found when welcoming the heavenly messengers.

Meditation: Do I feel at peace? Am I doing God's will? What do I need to change in my life so that the way I live might more closely match God's will?

Prayer: God of peace and love, draw me more deeply into intimacy with you. Give me the courage to be true to myself. Guide my actions that they may always be in accordance with your divine will. Enable me to welcome others with gracious hospitality. Grant peace in my heart and in the world. For this I pray. Amen.

A New Identity

Readings: Gen 17:3-9; John 8:51-59

Scripture:
No longer shall you be called Abram;
    your name shall be Abraham,
    for I am making you the father of a host of nations.
        (Gen 17:5)

Reflection: Today's first reading offers us one of many examples where God transforms the lives of the faithful, bestowing and fulfilling promises, and enabling people to rise to their full potential.

God had promised to make Abram the father of a great nation (see Gen 12:2). Now, the promise becomes even more lavish, as God speaks not of one nation but of "a host of nations." This increase in blessings is marked by a new name, "Abraham." This name literally means "father of a host of nations"—a name that helped shape Abraham's identity. The lives of Abraham and Sarah were transformed by this encounter.

There are many parallels between Abraham's story and our own. We gain a new identity in baptism when we are anointed as members of Christ. Henceforth we are called Christians; we are members of the Body of Christ. This new name shapes the way that we lead our lives, calling us to greater compassion and unity.

We are reminded of our identity whenever we process forward for communion and hear the words: "The Body of Christ." St. Augustine liked to draw attention to the multiple levels of meaning of this term. He would ask people to see themselves as one of the many grains of wheat in the bread transformed on the altar. He would challenge them to become what they received. Our "Amen" acknowledges our identity as members of that body and our willingness to be at one with all other members of the Body of Christ. Just as the multiple grains of wheat have been baked together to form one bread, God brings us together to form one body.

The promise to Abraham and Sarah must have seemed outlandish. They were already of advanced age, and yet God was promising to give them descendants. God fulfilled those promises. Whenever our troubles seem hopeless, or when we struggle to be as one with others, we must remember that God fulfills promises. God took an active role in the lives of Abraham and Sarah, and God takes an active role in our lives through the power of the Holy Spirit.

Meditation: In what ways do I wish I could start over? Where is God leading me now? What blessings has God sent into my life?

Prayer: Loving God, send your Holy Spirit to refresh us. Make us alive once again. Guide us to the future that you have in store for us. Amen.

Actions Convince

Readings: Jer 20:10-13; John 10:31-42

Scripture:
If I do not perform my Father's works, do not believe me;
   but if I perform them, even if you do not believe me,
   believe the works, so that you may realize and understand
   that the Father is in me and I am in the Father.
   (John 10:37-38)

Reflection: Jesus is telling us very clearly in today's gospel that actions must be believed, even when words fail to convince. The evidence speaks for itself.

We can all think of situations when words might fail to convince: politicians who promise not to raise taxes, perpetually tardy people who promise that next time they will be on time, smokers who claim they can easily kick the habit, salespeople who claim that their product is the best ever. Sometimes we are wise to doubt the words we hear. Actions are far more convincing.

Consider the actions of one woman who lent her car to a coworker whom she barely knew. This coworker needed to drive her husband to a medical appointment in a city that was three hours away. Some people give anonymous gifts to those in need. Countless volunteers step forward to help during natural disasters. Some children offer their favorite toys to those who have less. Terry Fox, who had already lost one leg to cancer, attempted to run across Canada to raise money for cancer research before succumbing to cancer himself. So many people do extraordinary things. Their actions challenge us and give us hope. They are all signs that the reign of God has already begun in our midst.

As we near Holy Week, when we remember Jesus' journey to Jerusalem and his passion and death, the reality of his actions begins to sink in. Given Jesus' actions, there can be no doubt. There can be no doubt of the immensity of Jesus' love for us—or of the degree to which he would go to convince us of that love.

Meditation: Throughout Lent, many of us have given up foods that we like or have made an effort to devote more time to prayer or charitable works. How successful have we been? Have our efforts been credible and sincere? Let us make a renewed effort for the remainder of Lent.

Prayer: O God of love, your Son led us back to you through his life, death, resurrection, and ascension into glory. His actions spoke more loudly than words ever could. As I go about my daily chores today, grant me self-discipline, strength, and guidance. May my actions reflect the belief that I profess, that Jesus Christ is Lord. I ask this through Jesus your Son, in unity with the Holy Spirit. Amen.

Gather

Readings: Ezek 37:21-28; John 11:45-56

Scripture:
He [Caiaphus] prophesied that Jesus was going to die for
   the nation,
   and not only for the nation,
   but also to gather into one the dispersed children of God.
   (John 11:51b-52)

Reflection: In some ways, we are all like snowflakes. We are created by God, each of us beautiful and unique, but we are somewhat weak on our own. When snowflakes are gathered together into a snowball, strength and power are infinitely greater. A snowball can have impact where individual snowflakes could not. God wants us to be gathered together as one, like snowflakes in a snowball. Our parish communities are like large snowballs glittering in the sunshine, reflecting and refracting the light of Christ for all to see.

   In today's first reading, we hear that God will gather the children of Israel and make them one nation. Jesus calls us to a profound unity, one where we respect each others' differences, honor one another's qualities, and work together for the good of the community as a whole. We may need to find the courage to gently admonish one another and the humility to accept the correction of others for the good of all.

Being one means getting to know one another enough to support one another. We need to move beyond a superficial niceness in order to genuinely care for one another. Christianity is a profoundly communal religion, where the goal is not just your salvation or my salvation, but the salvation of all.

Without Christ, this unity would not be possible. We cannot engineer unity on our own, but we can earnestly pray for unity and can cooperate as God offers us opportunities to come together. The process began with Christ's death and resurrection. We experience a foretaste of that oneness whenever we say yes to God's call to gather for worship.

Meditation: Have I taken the time to get to know the people with whom I worship? Do I pray for them and support them? How could we more truly be one?

Prayer: God of the covenant, you continue to gather us together, to make us one. Heal the church of all that divides us. May we truly become one. Grant us the courage, the wisdom, and the right vocabulary to gently and effectively address those issues that continue to separate us. May your kingdom come. Amen.

Mocking

Readings: Luke 19:28-40; Isa 50:4-7; Phil 2:6-11; Luke 22:14–23:56

Scripture:
Herod and his soldiers treated him contemptuously and
    mocked him,
    and after clothing him in resplendent garb,
    he sent him back to Pilate.
Herod and Pilate became friends that very day,
    even though they had been enemies formerly.
        (Luke 23:11-12)

Reflection: A well-respected high school principal needed to discipline two rowdy students. Other punishments had failed to change their behavior, so this time the principal forbade the students from going on a school trip. A little while later, as a form of revenge, these two students came forward to police with allegations that this principal had touched them inappropriately. He was charged with sexual assault and suspended from his job as principal. Even after the two students subsequently recanted and admitted that their allegations were false, criminal charges proceeded on the assumption that somebody must have pressured the young people to change their story. The press went to town on this poor man, destroying his reputation and negatively affecting his health. Many people in the small town believed the allegations and joined in the gossip. The principal couldn't even go into the grocery store without people pointing and whispering. Few people seemed to consider that he might indeed be innocent.

There is a danger that, like Herod and Pilate, mocking others is still an activity that brings people together and causes friendships to form. Children do this in the schoolyard. Adults sometimes act this way as well. To be with the in crowd, whatever that crowd might be, we join in mocking innocent bystanders. Let us pray for greater wisdom to recognize these instances, and let us take comfort in the generous words of Jesus: "Father, forgive them, they know not what they do" (Luke 23:34).

Meditation: Do I ever join in doing the wrong thing in order to be popular? Do I ever go against my better judgment in order to gain friends? Am I too quick to believe the worst about others?

Prayer: God of infinite love, I can find no words to express my gratitude for the gift of your Son. I stand in awe. Grant me the wisdom to avoid participation in gossip, mocking, or any other activity that inflicts pain. Forgive the times that I have given in to such temptation. Comfort all those who suffer from the words or actions of others. I ask this in the name of Jesus, who died for my sins, and through the Holy Spirit, who brings comfort and wisdom. Amen.

April 2: Monday of Holy Week

The Love of Christ

Readings: Isa 42:1-7; John 12:1-11

Scripture:
You always have the poor with you, but you do not always
    have me. (John 12:8)

Reflection: There is an old saying that goes something like
this: "Come work for the church. The hours are long and the
pay is low, but the retirement benefits are out of this world."
One of my friends has this sign on her office wall.

The concept could reasonably be extended not only to
church employees but to all who follow Christ. Christians
are usually busy people. We see the poor and the homeless
and try to help in some way. We hear that people are suffering overseas, so we pray and sometimes send money. We
minister in our own communities, teaching children, welcoming visitors, preparing music, decorating the worship
space, and sharing our faith with those who come seeking.
We may be asked to help with collection counting, church
repairs, visiting shut-ins, comforting the grieving, or cooking
for the parish supper. We may eventually feel worn out. Who
has the time and energy for everything?

Whether our involvement is big or small, our energy will
indeed become depleted unless we are fueled by a deep love
of God. Being a Christian is not just about keeping busy, as

valuable as all these tasks may be. Being Christian is first and foremost about loving and being loved by Christ. Children are often taught a song that begins, "Jesus loves me, this I know." We need to remember and believe in that love. We also need to affirm our love for Jesus in return. We do this with our unconditional focus, our yes without hesitation, our putting Jesus first in our lives.

In today's gospel, Mary lavishly pours expensive oil over Jesus' feet, giving him her absolute undivided love and attention. She anoints his feet with costly, perfumed oil and risks ridicule by using her hair to dry Jesus' feet. Only prostitutes let their hair flow freely; respectable women kept it tied up. But hers is an act of love. Jesus defends her actions and does not dismiss them as excessive in any way.

When we take the time to be nourished by that experience of love through heartfelt prayer, we will be able to go forth with great energy and enthusiasm to do all that God intends.

Meditation: How do I express my love to Jesus? Do I hold anything back from Jesus? Spend a few minutes now expressing your love to Jesus.

Prayer: God of love, you draw us into relationship with you through your Son. Grant us the grace to love and adore him without hesitation. May we follow the example of Mary of Bethany and give Christ our undivided love and attention. Amen.

Self-giving Love

Readings: Isa 49:1-6; John 13:21-33, 36-38

Scripture:
Jesus answered,
   "It is the one to whom I hand the morsel after I have
      dipped it."
So he dipped the morsel and took it and handed it to Judas,
   son of Simon the Iscariot. (John 13:26)

Reflection: Sadly, few of us go through life without feeling betrayed at some point or other. A young girl may confide in her best friend that she really likes a certain boy in class, and later she feels mortified when her friend tells that same boy this secret. How humiliating! A politician may make certain promises to obtain our votes—and then behave quite differently after elected. Is that not a betrayal?

Knowing how painful it is to be betrayed by someone whom we trust, we can perhaps imagine how painful it must have been for Jesus. Judas was one of his followers, a companion on the journey, somebody who had listened to his teachings and spent much time with him. And yet Jesus knew that Judas would be the one to betray him. He knew that this would happen according to God's plan.

The morsel that Jesus takes and gives to Judas reminds us of the Eucharist. Even at this moment of pain, faced with somebody who will surely betray him, Jesus the Living Bread shares bread with Judas. What an example of self-giving love! Can we be as generous to those who seek to harm us? Yes, with God's grace we can.

There continues to be evil in the world, and we still encounter people who try our patience, annoy us—and even some who seek to harm us. When we are in situations where we must interact regularly with such people, how do we respond? It can be very difficult to be kind and respectful toward a person we do not trust, especially if that person has harmed us or others in the past and continues to be a risk. Such situations suggest the need for both prayers and caution. When interacting with such individuals, we may be tempted to respond with hostility. Jesus models for us a better approach—a demonstration of love and respect.

Meditation: Have I ever betrayed a friend or revealed a confidence? Have I repented and sought forgiveness? When I am with those whom I distrust, how do I respond?

Prayer: God of mercy and love, your Son Jesus gives us the ultimate example of love, even in the face of betrayal. Forgive the times that I have betrayed others or that I have not treated others with love and respect. Give me the grace to be able to model Christ's love to all whom I encounter this day. Send forth your Spirit to renew the face of the earth and to transform the hearts of those who seek to do evil. For this I earnestly pray. Amen.

April 4: Wednesday of Holy Week

A Word to Rouse Them

Readings: Isa 50:4-9a; Matt 26:14-25

Scripture:
The Lord GOD has given me
   a well-trained tongue,
That I might know to speak to the weary
   a word that will rouse them.
Morning after morning
   he opens my ear that I may hear;
And I have not rebelled,
   have not turned back. (Isa 50:4-5)

Reflection: On December 1, 1955, Rosa Parks refused to give up her seat on a bus in Montgomery, Alabama. That simple, non-violent protest by a well-respected seamstress was a key step in the battle against racial segregation in the American South. Parks no doubt suffered for her decision, but her protest was successful. Her arrest triggered a boycott of the Montgomery bus system—and ultimately the end of segregation. At the time of her funeral in 2005, thousands of people turned out to honor the courage of this fine lady.

In today's first reading, commonly known as one of the Suffering Servant songs, we see another person reflecting on the experience of speaking out. This person speaks effectively, eloquently, and encouragingly as a disciple who has learned his lessons well. But he is not heard. He suffers violence for his words, and yet he perseveres.

Everyday, someone, somewhere in the world, is standing up to prejudice, racism, or other injustices. These people have a deep sense of outrage in the face of injustice. Sometimes, they suffer for their convictions, losing friends, feeling ostracized, or in the case of today's first reading, being beaten and spat on. Yet somehow they have the strength to persevere. Frequently, they are heard.

Jesus also called on people to hear a message of good news. And he suffered and died for his convictions. But through the Resurrection, the effect of his courageous actions changed our world beyond anyone's wildest dreams. Many people did not listen, and some still do not listen, but more are coming to Christ every day. Some in our very midst are preparing to experience new life in Christ through the waters of baptism. Thanks be to God.

Meditation: In what ways am I being called to speak out about injustice? Would I be willing to risk my personal comfort in order to do the right thing? Do I listen when others try to open my eyes to injustice?

Prayer: O God of justice, bless all who continue Christ's work here on earth, challenging injustice and teaching the Good News. Give us all the wisdom to know when you are calling us to act, the courage to respond, and the words to speak. Open our ears when others try to make us hear. We ask this through Christ our Lord. Amen.

A Note about the Triduum

We begin a new chapter today. Lent ends near sundown this evening, before we begin our celebration of the Evening Mass of the Lord's Supper. Let us pause and collect our thoughts before crossing the threshold into the most holy time in the church calendar: the Sacred Triduum.

For forty days, God has been forming us, calling us to reflect on the way we lead our lives, and challenging us to compare our present individual and collective reality with the vision that God offers us. The triune God has been acting in our lives, calling us to repentance, guiding our thoughts, and sustaining our efforts. We have fasted, we have repented, and we have experienced reconciliation.

But now the time for preparation is past; the time for basking in the mystery is upon us. During these days our liturgical rituals draw us deeply into the transformative power of Christ's death and resurrection.

As we look ahead to the activities of these next three days, we notice their unity. Even though the tone and ambience of each day is distinct, there is a unifying thread as we unfold different facets of the death and resurrection of Christ. Holy Thursday and Good Friday already contain hints that point to resurrection joy. Time stands still for us, and these three days are as one. There is no dismissal after the Evening Mass of the Lord's Supper or after the Good Friday Celebration of the Lord's Passion, nor is there an opening greeting on

Good Friday or at the Easter Vigil. The liturgies simply flow together as one liturgy, as one unified experience.

Triduum is a time of retreat for the entire church, a time to spend with God, a time like no other. Together we reflect upon the greatest mysteries of our faith and willingly participate in profound transformation. This transformation makes us look forward to the renewal of our baptismal vows at the Easter Vigil, and to the joyous, life-giving sprinkling of baptismal water upon the whole community. We look forward as well to witnessing the baptisms of new members of the Body of Christ. Our thoughts and prayers go out to those who will be baptized throughout the world, and we offer praise to God.

Let us immerse ourselves wholeheartedly in the experience of Triduum, knowing that we will soon be singing Alleluia!

April 5: Holy Thursday (Maundy Thursday)

Personal Connection

Readings: Exod 12:1-8, 11-14; 1 Cor 11:23-26; John 13:1-15

Scripture:
He took a towel and tied it around his waist.
Then he poured water into a basin
and began to wash the disciples' feet
and dry them with the towel around his waist.
(John 13:4b-5)

Reflection: On Monday, we heard the story of Mary of Bethany anointing Jesus' feet and then drying them with her hair. Today we hear of Jesus washing the disciples' feet and then drying them with a towel that had been tied around his waist. Both actions show a close personal connection.

After washing their feet, Jesus goes on to tell the disciples that they should also wash one another's feet. To show that we have heard this call to be of service to one another, some parishes have a custom of collecting food for the food shelves this evening. Parishioners bring canned goods as a reminder that they are aware of their obligation to assist others. As noble as such a gesture may be as a first step, is today's gospel not calling us to something more?

Our duty is not complete when we offer canned goods or give a little money. Our duty is complete only when we connect personally with others, showing that we recognize their dignity and worth. Such actions require far greater investment of our time and our emotions.

Some early Christian communities washed the feet of the newly baptized as a sign of their personal connection with Christ and with the Christian community. Foot washing is a humbling action that breaks down barriers, reminding us of the very human needs that we share. As we experience foot-washing in our worship this evening, may the sound and sight of pouring water remind us of our own baptisms and of the baptisms that many will experience at the Easter Vigil. May we, as heirs of Christ, recognize our personal connection with Christ and with one another. May we be one.

Meditation: How is God calling me to be attentive to the needs of others? The disciples were changed by their encounter with Christ. How have I been changed?

Prayer: Jesus, you humbled yourself to do a very loving deed for your disciples. Grant us the humility to accept your love and to be loving, caring servants to one another. Amen.

Come, Let us Worship

Readings: Isa 52:13–53:12; Heb 4:14-16; 5:7-9; John 18:1–19:42

Scripture:
Jesus, knowing everything that was going to happen to him,
   went out and said to them, "Whom are you looking for?"
They answered him, "Jesus the Nazorean."
He said to them, "I AM."
Judas his betrayer was also with them.
When he said to them, "I AM,"
   they turned away and fell to the ground. (John 18:4-6)

Reflection: We all experience suffering at some point in our life, and so we are able to relate to the power of today's passion narrative, no matter how many times we have heard the story before. At times, the burdens of life may lead us to a dark place spiritually and psychologically, a place from which hope seems absent and where it is a struggle to even pray. However, even in the darkest moments of our lives, there is hope. God is always there, and there are signs of hope if we can only see them. There are also profound signs of hope in today's liturgy.

During the veneration rite, the priest sings, "This is the wood of the cross, on which hung the Savior of the world." We respond, "Come, let us worship." These words deserve to be pondered carefully. Whenever we worship, we praise and glorify God with love and gratitude. Therefore, we gaze on and venerate the wood of the cross, humbled by the magnitude of God's love for the whole world. We know that Christ's gift ushered in the beginning of a new era, an age characterized by love, healing, joy, and an end to divisions. For Jesus, and ultimately for us as well, death will lead to resurrection.

John's passion account tells us that Jesus is very much in control. He is taking the initiative. The guards and soldiers fall to the ground in homage, recognizing Jesus as the Son of God. This entire passion event took place with Jesus' full cooperation. He suffered an excruciating, humiliating death, but he did so willingly, such was his love for us. Jesus announced, "It is finished" (John 19:30), and he surrendered his life as a gift to God.

Even while he was still on the cross, Jesus gave us reason to hope. When the soldier's spear pierced Jesus' side, blood and water flowed, the same blood that is now in our communion cup and the same life-giving water that we find in the baptismal font. Jesus' actions opened the way to salvation. Come, let us worship.

Meditation: Are my eyes open to see the signs of hope even in the midst of suffering? Do I surrender my life into God's hands? Let us pause in silence to marvel at the enormity of Christ's gift and the unfathomable impact that it has had—and continues to have—in our lives and in our world.

Prayer: Ever-merciful God, the gift of your Son surpasses my comprehension. Grant that I may never forget and never cease to be grateful for Jesus' gift of self. For this I pray, through Jesus, who gave his life for the salvation of the world. Amen.

Presence Among the Dead

Reflection: It seems good that there is a gap between Good Friday and Easter Sunday, for there is usually a time lag in our own lives between the source of suffering and our gradual return to new life. If we are mourning the death of a loved one or coming to terms with distressing news, seldom is it helpful to hear somebody tell us to "get over it" or "get on with life." We need time to process our experience and to adjust to our new reality.

Suffering can be very isolating. Sometimes the isolation is physical, as when the sick are homebound. At other times, the isolation can be emotional, such as when pride or shame prevent us from even admitting our problem. Maybe our pain is so great that we struggle to find words to express it, and so we choose to remain silent. At such times, the comforting and supportive presence of someone who knows us well may be exactly what we need. Such people compassionately offer to listen, but do not insist that we carry on a conversation. This is the pastoral ministry of presence.

In the Apostle's Creed, we profess our belief that Jesus "descended to the dead." Jesus continues to enter into the dark space of our suffering, being present to us, offering us hope, but not rushing us. Jesus can be present to us because he has shared our experience. His love for us was so great that he wanted to experience the fullness of our humanity.

He knows what it feels like to suffer, to feel alienated and alone. That experience makes it possible for us to approach Jesus in our despair and to welcome his presence.

Yesterday we heard the acclamation, "This is the wood of the cross, on which hung the Savior of the world." Christ was and is the Savior of the world, whose grace is accessible to all, across time and space. Part of Christ's time among the dead was spent proclaiming the Good News of salvation to those who had gone before (see 1 Peter 3:19). No one was out of the reach of the saving power of the cross. Icons depict Christ breaking the doors of hell, grasping the wrists of Adam and Eve and lifting them victoriously toward heaven. Adam and Eve do nothing to help; their salvation, like ours, is a gift from God in the person of Jesus.

Meditation: Whom do I know that is suffering? Might my understanding presence bring them some comfort? How might I be the light of Christ for those who stand in darkness?

Prayer: Holy and anointed Lord, words fail to express my awe and gratitude when I ponder how you suffered for the salvation of the world. You experienced betrayal, pain, suffering, and alienation. Comfort all those who suffer today. Show me how I can be a source of comfort and hope to those who suffer. I look with longing toward this evening, when we will once again celebrate your resurrection. In awe and gratitude, I pray. Amen.

A Fresh Start

Readings: Acts 10:34a, 37-43; Col 3:1-4 or 1 Cor 5:6b-8; John 20:1-9

Scripture:
Clear out the old yeast,
  so that you may become a fresh batch of dough,
  inasmuch as you are unleavened.
For our paschal lamb, Christ, has been sacrificed. (1 Cor 5:7)

Reflection: In preparation for Passover, the custom is to remove all products made from old yeast, not only from the diet, but from the house. All traces of bread are to be eliminated. A spring cleaning activity ensures that not a crumb remains, creating a decisive break with one's old diet and an openness to something new. At the time of the Exodus, the Jewish people left Egypt hastily and could not wait for bread to rise, so they ate unleavened bread. Passover reenacts this flight from Egypt, this departure from slavery and embrace of new life.

The shift from slavery to freedom was not merely external. Their attitudes also needed to shift, as they learned once again what it meant to be free, to make decisions, to willingly assume certain obligations, and to act with dignity.

Throughout our Lenten journey, we have reflected on many dimensions of slavery and bondage in our lives. We reflected on addressing bad habits, weaknesses, broken relationships, selfish tendencies, and other aspects of sin that we wish to leave behind. Now, we have arrived at the moment when we experience new life. The past is past, and we are now ready to embrace something totally new: Jesus is risen! Alleluia! We have been set free.

May this moment touch our hearts so that we grasp this truth at a very deep level of our being. Many parishes celebrate baptisms today and throughout the Easter season, and we take delight in this tangible witness of new life in Christ. We see and hear many other signs of new life: cheerful faces and bright smiles, joyful music and voices raised in song, the light of the paschal candle and the waters of baptism. We are overjoyed. We feel blessed. We feel free. We begin anew.

Meditation: What signs of new life do I see? Let us pause and bask in the joy of this day, as we give thanks and praise to God for setting us free from the bonds of sin through the power of the Resurrection.

Prayer: O risen Christ, we glorify your name and give you praise! Alleluia! Alleluia! You are risen indeed! As we contemplate the mystery of your resurrection, show us how we can sustain the fervor and joy we feel this day. Strengthen us and guide us. In your name we pray. Alleluia! Amen.

Reference

The image of the salmon in the Ash Wednesday reflection was previously published in *Celebrate!*: Sherri Vallee, "Ash Wednesday," *Celebrate!* 42 (March–April 2003) 35–37.